Handmade Houses:
A Guide to the Woodbutcher's Art

Handmade Houses

A Guide to
the Woodbutcher's Art

Art Boericke / Barry Shapiro

Scrimshaw Press

1973

This book is dedicated to
the builders and their old ladies
&
To Susan
for giving more
than she received.

© 1973 by Arthur Boericke. All rights reserved.
Library of Congress Catalog Card Number: 73-78445
ISBN: 0-912020-00-8
Printed in the United States of America
Fifth printing, December, 1973

The Scrimshaw Press
149 Ninth Street
San Francisco
California 94103

Foreword

FOR SOME YEARS we have heard the extravagant technological promise of housing at low cost. It has never come to pass. The answer to low cost housing, it seems to me, is to make a break with a "standard of living" that makes us slaves to centralized decision-making and control, to an economy whose values are the magnitude of production and consumption. The dollar is not a reasonable measure of the quality of life or the quality of place.

Yet most of us are still children of that dollar, and of the institutions we grew up in—we are conditioned to their ways. For most of us have grown up sharing little real experience or work. We have few rituals that celebrate our unity of body, mind and spirit. We are trying to find our way back into the earth family and there are few guides to show the way.

Thus, one of our tasks is to repair the rift between our "objective" and our "subjective" selves, to unite the division between the inner and outer man, a division nurtured by the machine metaphor, by the separation of one's work from one's identity. A division aided by fragmentation of our time, and by the physical settings that support this split. Getting myself together started with getting my time and space into one place, with creating the possibility and essential conditions for that wholeness.

This day I chiseled four mortise joints to receive the tenoned posts that will be the frame of our sauna. In fourteen years of architectural practice I never designed a mortise and tenon joint because it was too much handwork and at carpenter's wages, far too expensive. So now I am learning to make them myself.

It is taking me a long time to get over the guilt of spending days hard at work learning to do the things I wasn't trained to do. It is taking a long time to accept simple satisfaction of doing what I am doing, living in the present.

Sim Van der Ryn,
The School of Architecture,
University of California, Berkeley

Preface

I DON'T REGRET having worked with union carpenters and union plumbers and union electricians—far from it. I wouldn't have stayed in the trades some twenty years if I had. Yet I do regret the shoddy, unimaginative work that we do in order to earn a living in the trades.

So, eight years ago, working on weekends only, I started to build myself a home. It was not a house that the bank or a run-of-the-mill contractor would consider prudent or resaleable. It was a place salvaged from remodeling and demolition jobs, a place pieced together from flea markets and country dumps—but a good-sized place built out on the southern slope of a little hogback where it caught the morning sun and rising moon.

And thus, despite a dozen years of ticky-tacky building, I was getting a little jump on things; I'd begun a home that was suited to the way I actually lived—the way I slept and breathed and worked. In short, a solid little shed that had some of the spirit and the personality of the builder busting through. But if I was proud of its uniqueness it was, all the same, a place that could very well be duplicated by almost any greenhorn or apprentice who showed any aptitude at all.

Only five years later, when I began looking about for other homes built pretty much like mine, I had to admit that the ingenuity of many of the newcomers had gone far past my own. For, no mistaking it, building their own place had become the four-square gospel for scores of young rambunctious dudes. In fact, a lot of compact, hardy little places had started up and there were craftsmen making do with salvaged lumber, hand-hewn beams, adobe bricks, and redwood thatch all along the upland creeks and logging flats and steep ravines. And these places showed such spontaneity that I could barely understand the builders' diverse ways of doing things at first.

No indeed, we old-timers weren't the only ones dodging the inspectors anymore and though that was gratifying in its way, it was damned perplexing too. For the changes had tumbled everything we'd slowly and painfully learnt—thrown among the skittering enthusiasms and youthful glee that bobbed up everywhere we went.

So I don't aim to explain all these new places, not even those I worked on—and I'm not sure I could. If you learn anything at all from glancing through this book, then instead of the cheerless little rooms you may have been sketching for your dreamhouse, you might just start in and build yourself a good-sized country kitchen and let it go at that. (Relax, just live in it a while before you build an alcove or a sleeping platform or a separate bunkhouse for the kids. And then relax some more before you build a bath or sauna.)

But there I go—don't let me influence *your* way of doing it, for what gets worked on first is for some a matter of convenience and for others more a matter of tradition—the Scandinavians start in with the sauna, live there a while, and then set up the home and the barns. So let it grow. Just get a start and let it grow.

Consult *The Old Farmer's Almanac*, or Second Corinthians, or the *I Ching*, but keep right on with it. And if the inspectors come around, call your place a "potting shed," a "summer camp," or "mining claim"—anything that pops into your head. And when they keep on shoving, call it a "firehouse," a "briar patch," a "commune" —whatever riles them most. If they take to threatening you, you can demand a jury trial and that will hold them off a while. (Out here they've lost their cases two times out of three in court, and the fines they collect the one time don't pay their costs.)

Consequently, depending on how you size them up, you can enter the courthouse declaiming, "life, liberty, and the pursuit of happiness!" or crying "up free enterprise!" and "law and order!" For remember, they can't disconnect you from the utilities you're not installing—you being an ecology freak, a joyous monk, or an ornery young codger like me. And remember, too, property is sacred; so if we just keep on building, they're going to step aside—see if they don't. Sure, we may be poor, but—as they say in Texas—"our heels are square," and that's what counts,

Of that I'm certain,
Art Boericke

SOME OF THESE places were sixty miles up a dirt road and five miles further and once we got to them, some were just too small or too well-hidden to photograph at all. Moreover, one burned down before we got to it and another was demolished by the *Coast Guard*. So we can't say we got *everything* we might have, but possibly we got more than we could reasonably have hoped for, even if we weren't able to do justice to every place we visited— especially those that were four miles up a creek, or those we came upon when it was raining. At least the greeting was almost always as frank and open as this young lady's . . .

I SUPPOSE THAT this builder isn't the first to approach a music studio in this fashion, but this place certainly drops the usual way of getting things together, to bob up with a syncopated pattern more in keeping with the ragas played within it.

BUILT BY A retired engineer who worked the logs into place himself with a block and tackle, this woodland cabin is a mighty educated but joyous little place! It's a pleasure just walking down the path and up the driftwood stairs—which only goes to show that some engineers are really artists, just like the rest of us.

IT SURE TAKES time to find all the doors and beams and siding when it's salvage that you're after, but it beats calling up the lumberyard and getting wood that has no character to it. Besides, these pieces from a dentist's office, a shipyard, an army barracks and a high school gym would have made just so much scrap without someone, like myself, using them again.

A FISHING SHACK that was altered a bit inside with odds and ends
that came floating down the river and then had a little deck and
a bay window tacked on too. If you're going to renovate at all,
you might as well get in and really do the job, not just tinker with it.

DINING, BATH, AND BEDROOMS form separate
units here in order to provide each room with
more light, better ventilation, and soundproofing that's economical.
And building it this way also makes it easier to heat. A very
down-home arrangement—natural, cheap and practical.

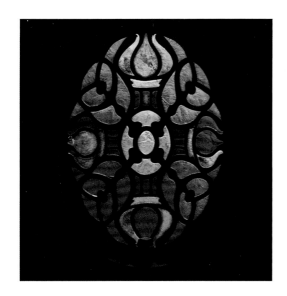

A LARGER more elaborate place filled with cheerful bunks and
little nooks in addition to a certain amount of just plain idle space.
And though it's been set up to buffer the owner from the commotion
of her kids and to entertain a lot of people, it hasn't any stiffness
or formality in its dignified design.

A woodsy little place with lots of "charm"—or maybe "joy" would be a better word. It's been put together by local craftsmen who show their rambunctious personalities in every beam and shake and every door and window.

. . . The sort of room that's bright and cheerful in the sun, but equally good in fog or overcast, by the light of flickering candles or the autumn moon.

No place should be all eyes like Argus—unless it's buried deep
within the woods. And even then, if it's a trifle large inside it can be
hard to heat, though that's possibly not too high a price for living
in a zany place like this.

OPEN CITY! The builder likes it that way and so do I . . . and several goats and chickens like it too.

A VERY SNUG, well-crafted, trim and spunky little place that sits
right into its hogback with a jaunty air that's pretty much in keeping
with the pennant flying in the morning breeze. It illustrates what
Sir Henry Wotton meant when he said, 350 years ago, "Well
building hath three conditions—commodity, firmness, and delight."

A SCULPTOR built this one with salvage, but with carefully selected, well-cured wood for his tables, benches, and even his stools.

ACTUALLY, two buildings are pictured here—the exterior of one and
the interior of another. The sleeping cabin is more in a down-country
or rural style, but the dining shack's a bit more citified with its
painted walls and hardwood floor. Yet with its bunk up overhead
it seems to fit in with its rough-hewn neighbor.

BY FAR the handsomest A-frame I've ever seen and a place that illustrates the great feeling that comes from details that speak of genuine love and craftsmanship. In building, as in other things, you get pretty much what you put into it.

A PIRATE'S ROOST built by a youngster who eased up on the local practice of building almost entirely with adobe, for his steep ravine wouldn't quite accommodate that sort of weight.

AND ANOTHER PROJECT by a youngster, a stump house. Perhaps everyone has dreamt of living in a tree sometime or other, but few have actually done it with such style as this.

ONE OF THE OLD-TIMERS, and still the undisputed champion when it comes to an almost medieval atmosphere of well-scaled pomp and power—yet it isn't actually half as big as it seems when you walk in the door.

ANOTHER HEAVYWEIGHT place, fitted together from bridge
timbers that have been notched out with the owner's chainsaw! It
has an almost religious quality to it, although, for its size, it's
one of the cheapest places standing.

THERE IS A surprising number of well-built little octagons popping up in the woods these days—most of them almost as handsome and livable as this one here. All are a little tight on space unless you're an expert at compartmentalizing things —especially children's toys and stuff.

ONCE THE FOUNDATION and the rough framing were in, the owner's
teenage son came on the job and finished up the shingling. Then he
ducked inside and just kept on moving. Which isn't a bad way to
go if you haven't the experience or confidence it takes for doing a
fairly complex sort of home like this.

HERE'S AN EXAMPLE of what you can do with not much more than a hammer and an axe. Plus, of course, a little imagination.

THIS CRAFTSMAN'S trade, pottery, has influenced his way of
building—no doubt of that. And it's left him with not much
time or money for finishing the roof. As some contractors are apt
to say, "It's sort of weathering in."

THIS PLACE is as nearly perfect as any place can be, for this builder does *all* the work himself, whether it's carving stone, making bricks, dapping timbers, or even fashioning the hardware for the doors.

AND BEING a sculptor he makes use of every twist and turn, every tree and stone, so that the house seems to *grow* around the boulders instead of being built around them.

PRETTY DAMN GOOD for just $800 in materials, especially with all that glass. And somehow the little balcony perches up there without giving the place a crowded feeling. It's all in knowing how, or mostly so. The rest is work.

An A-frame that's stood the test of time and made good use of cement asbestos boards, a difficult material to set off in any style. But again, little details make all the difference—details and craftsmanship.

CEMENT, old windshields, some colored glass, a little carving on the door and you have a big newfangled solarium for plants or bathing or anything you like.

LOOKING DOWN from logging cables, a new-world tea house hovers over a swiftly-flowing stream.

A WOODSHED converted to a playhouse and . . .

A TREEHOUSE, complete with running water.

TABLES AND CHAIRS and rockers and stairs can all be put together in more ways than one.

A CHICKEN COOP and a couple of old-time privies—

TWO SAUNAS. Here's another case where lots of savvy and a little craftsmanship sure make a difference in both utility and joy.

KITCHENS ARE the heart of any home, so here are some that are neither too fussy, too polished, nor too antiseptic for whipping up a country meal.

AND THERE'S a country stove for every pocketbook, including one just built to order by a welder who happened by.

A LITTLE PLACE to get away from things or practice yoga—what
you might call a meditation room with roots. And then a much more
formal one that's been caught in the first light of breaking day.

A BEDROOM in the woods and a workshop
—usually what us woodbutchers would
like to put up first thing but get to doing
last.

THIS SORT of carving was common once around all sorts of doors and gables; but it takes a lot of talent, and a lot of time as well . . .

A BARN that was built by casting dice. After the principal posts were chosen and positioned on an ancient oracle's advice, the work was beautifully completed by budding Buddhist monks.

WALLS, FENCES, GATES . . .

EVEN SOME architects can use a saw, but the result is usually not
as well-done as this. There's just no substitute for doing it yourself.

A Word

FROM THE PHOTOGRAPHER: I like to photograph people, so
architectural photography normally does not interest me. Yet the
very first of these owner-crafted homes Art took me to, though
empty at that moment, was just *alive* with people! Out flew
all notions of right-angle, make-it-look-better-than-it-is,
super flash photography. For the next three years Art and I knocked
around the countryside, sleeping on the ground, getting wet,
walking a lot and carrying a minimum of equipment—a $2\frac{1}{4}$ format
camera, a few lenses, and usually too little film—just meeting some
fine people (who'd like to remain anonymous, insisting that their
homes speak for them). I hope you *feel* their presence, as I will
always feel their presence in every beam and rafter, every
latch and piece of hardware.

Barry Shapiro

We made a fifth printing of this book in December, 1973,
with color separations by Gregory & Falk, printing by Phelps-Schaefer
and binding by Stecher-Cardoza.
The type is Intertype Medieval, with Goudy
and Hearst display, set by Mercury
Typography Co. and Solotype.
The paper is 100# Centura Dull.
Production by Karen Petersen
and Richard Schuettge, design by Frederick Mitchell
and Judith Whipple.